PHILIP KNIGHT

Running

with

Nike

PHILIP KNIGHT

Running

with

Nike

David R. Collins

GEC GARRETT EDUCATIONAL CORPORATION

Cover photo: *Philip Knight.* (Rich Iwasaki.)

Edited and produced by Synthegraphics Corporation

Library of Congress Cataloging in Publication Data

Collins, David R.
    Philip H. Knight—running with Nike / David R. Collins.
      p. cm. — (Wizards of business)
    Includes index.
    Summary: Describes how entrepreneur Philip Knight developed the
successful Nike company.
    ISBN 1-56074-020-5
    1. Knight, Philip H., 1938- —Juvenile literature.
2. Businessmen—United States—Biography—Juvenile literature.
3. Sporting goods industry—United States—History—Juvenile
literature.   4. Nike (Firm)—History—Juvenile literature.
[1. Knight, Philip H., 1938-   .   2. Businessmen.   3. Nike (Firm)—
History.]   I. Title.   II. Series.
HD9992.U52K553   1991
338.7′6887′092—dc20   91-32316
[B]   CIP
                                                                AC

Contents

Chronology for **Philip Knight**

1938	Born on February 24 in Portland, Oregon
1955	Entered University of Oregon; joined track team coached by Bill Bowerman
1959	Received bachelor's degree in business administration
1959–1960	Served with U.S. Army Transportation Corps
1962	Received master's degree from Stanford University
1963	Formed Blue Ribbon Sports in partnership with Bill Bowerman
1967–1969	Taught business administration at Portland State University
1968	Married Penelope Parks on September 13
1971	Introduced Nike as a product name
1981	Nike International, Ltd., formed
1982	Named Oregon Businessman of the Year
1986	Nike revenues topped the billion-dollar mark
1989	Introduced "Just Do It!" campaign; named Man of the Year by *Footwear News*
1990	Operation PUSH threatened boycott of Nike products

Chapter 1

Inside the Michael Jordan Building

$\mathbf{A}$mong the busiest workers at the new Nike corporate complex in Beaverton, Oregon, are the research technicians in the sparkling, modern Michael Jordan Building. Inside the Nike (pronounced Ni-key) Sports Research Laboratory, which is located in the Jordan Building, highly trained individuals devote their efforts to produce the best all-around shoe for professional athletes and would-be pros as well.

Nike's spacious laboratory resembles a "Star Wars" setting, with every kind of gadget and machinery needed to test the strength and durability of a Nike shoe. One machine smashes a shoe against all sorts of surfaces a person might run on, analyzing how the shoe's sole would stand up on stone or asphalt, on wood or artificial turf. In another area of the laboratory, video cameras are set up to film the reaction of a Nike shoe running along an ever-moving treadmill.

One of the most sophisticated devices in the laboratory is a force platform. Here, electronic sensors detect the amount of force exerted by a foot in action, whether it is leaping into the air or kicking a ball.

WHAT TO EXPECT FROM A SHOE

"Just how much can you expect from a shoe?" one might ask.

That's exactly what Philip Knight, the co-founder of Nike, and his experts want to find out. Already they have discovered and patented the Air-Sole, the Footbridge Stabilizer, and the Dynamic Fit system. But there's always a concept that has not been explored. How about Air 180 that is now being studied? This is a super-charged running shoe that contains fifty percent more air in its sole. It also has a window that allows a 180-degree side view and a complete bottom view of the air pocket in the shoe's heel. And not far behind is a shoe with an entire air-filled sole. Unbelievable!

Is It Worth It?

There are those who might charge Nike with overdoing it. After all, the majority of its customers are not Michael Jordans. There is the English teacher in Moline, Illinois, who simply enjoys a Wednesday night game of basketball in the school gym with his colleagues. Or maybe it's the business executive in Southfield, Michigan, who likes to swat a tennis ball around on weekends. Just how much do they need from a shoe? Is it worth all the time, effort, and money Nike pours into its products?

Whether the Nike shoes are aimed at the professional athlete or the amateur "jock," Philip Knight demands constant attention to quality, style, and performance of his products. (Rich Iwasaki.)

"You bet it is!" declares Philip Knight, who believes that proper shoes are especially important for the non-professional athlete. "The pros regiment their lives to their sports, watching what they eat, how much sleep they're getting, a regular exercise program. Sure, we want to offer them the best equipment we can so they can excel. But the average individual, enjoying a sport as a recreation, may not be in the best physical condition. He still wants to get the most out of himself. Naturally, I'm talking about women as well. They all want to do their best. It's up to us to assist by offering them the very best of equipment—equipment that is safe, sturdy and stylish."

Stealing Nikes

It's the "style" that has brought Nike a great deal of criticism. "$125 for a pair of sneakers! Ridiculous!" parents have been heard to complain. Sadly enough, because of their high cost, some individuals have been known to steal for a pair of Nikes. Such an awareness saddens Philip Knight and his people.

"Naturally, we try to put together the best products we can," offers one Nike **spokesperson.** (Terms in **boldface type** are defined in the Glossary at the back of this book.) "Our **marketing** and advertising people promote our **merchandise** in a positive, creative way. We're proud of what we make and want our customers to know what they are getting. As far as our prices go, it's a matter of paying to get the best on the **market.** Quality costs. It always has and it always will. As for the lawbreakers, let's keep the blame where it belongs—on those individuals. If a man steals a Cadillac, you don't blame the manufacturer."

Welcoming New Ideas

Philip Knight is the type of company manager who allows his team a lot of freedom. Ideas for new products come from anywhere, and he encourages creative thinking.

When a Nike worker brought in a teddy bear one day and stepped on it, he quickly encouraged his co-workers to do the same. The feeling was like being on a trampoline made of sponge. More teddy bears were ordered, cut up, and made into shoes. Before long, Nike entered into a **contract** with Mattel, the giant toy maker that manufactured the substance Phylon for use in its teddy bears. Soon Phylon-based running and hiking shoes were rolling off the Nike production lines.

Not that every Nike product works. The company's basketball pump shoe, put out in 1990, trailed far behind the pump-design model put out by Reebok, one of Nike's chief **competitors.** The major difference was that Reebok's model offered a self-contained pump; Nike's had a separate device for pumping air into the shoe cuff.

"Our model was aimed at basketball players with ankle problems," explained one Nike official. "We were trying to fill a particular need, not add a major product suited to everyone's needs."

COMPANY CHEERLEADER

Nonetheless, had the Nike pump shoe caught on, it would have surely brightened the faces of company executives, including Philip Knight. Creating a winner provides cause for celebration throughout the organization. Knight is famed as his company's best cheerleader, being the first to congratulate top technicians and workers for their successes.

Even at sales pep meetings, Knight is known for becoming watery-eyed and emotional when discussing Nike. "Our company revolves around people, products and principles," he asserts, "each working in context with each other."

A DIFFERENT TYPE OF EXECUTIVE

Philip Knight is hardly the typical corporate executive. He is willing to don appropriate businessman attire for those occasions that demand it. But the youthful-looking Knight feels more comfortable in a beard, open-neck shirt, jeans, and a pair of Nikes minus socks. A longtime running schedule has managed to keep unwanted and unneeded weight off his six-foot frame.

For Philip Knight, the Pacific Northwest has always been home. To him, this wonderful part of the country is a special place in which to dream and grow, to work and live, to start a company and raise a family. It is the setting for a marvelous success story that began over half a century ago.

Chapter 2

Knight's First Daylight

Thursday, February 24, 1938. Officially, it was still winter. But Mother Nature has seldom been known to pay attention to the calendar. On this particular morning, springlike breezes stirred the trees along the streets and avenues of Portland, Oregon. By noon, the temperature had reached quietly into the 40s with a light winter rain shower dampening the city. An hour away from the city, a peaceful Mt. Hood stretched its 11,235 feet of rock into the sky, like a watchful sentinel over the northwestern terrain.

ENTER PHILIP KNIGHT

The hearty cries of newborn infants were a familiar sound inside the Portland hospital. Certainly, the squawks and squeaks of the baby boy born to William and Lota Hatfield Knight were little different from those of others born on that particular February afternoon in Portland. But the proud parents rejoiced at the addition to their family—and hoped that their child would grow up in a peaceful world.

It was not an idle wish. Like most other Portland-area residents, William and Lota Knight kept a close watch on the news events of the day. Although the nation seemed to have pulled itself out of one major calamity, another appeared to be forming in the distance.

HARD TIMES IN AMERICA

"**Depression**." The word still causes Americans to wince in pain. Like millions of people across the country, the folks of Portland had enjoyed economic prosperity during the 1920s. Jobs were plentiful, wages good, and businesses flourished.

Then, without warning, on October 29, 1929, the American economy collapsed. **Investors** flooded their **brokers** with orders to sell their **stocks.** On that fateful October day, stock prices plummeted as over 13 million shares of stock changed hands.

Although most Americans did not understand exactly what had happened, they sensed that their own money might be in danger. Quickly, they began pulling their money out of banks and other financial institutions. Banks were forced to close, as were businesses that depended on loans from the banks. Workers were laid off, families were plunged into financial crisis. The 1930s were gloomy times for the people of Portland, including the William Knight family.

A Nation Recovers

Largely through the **policies** of President Franklin D. Roosevelt, the national economy began to recover by the late 1930s. After being sworn in as President in 1932, Roosevelt immediately started programs to rebuild America's financial institutions and to put people back to work. By the February day in 1938 when Philip Knight was born, the people of Portland and the rest of the United States were beginning to recover from the Depression.

War Clouds

But while the economy began to improve in America, war clouds were developing in other parts of the world. The pulse beats of Americans everywhere began to quicken as newspaper headlines announced

CZECHOSLOVAKIA PREPARES FOR WAR

In the story accompanying the headlines were the names of three men who were constantly in the news: German leader Adolph Hitler, Italy's Premier Benito Mussolini, and England's Prime Minister Neville Chamberlain. At a meeting with Chamberlain, Hitler and Mussolini claimed they only wanted peace. But while talking peace, Germany and Italy were building mighty armies and amassing huge collections of weapons.

Respected journalist E. B. White likened the meeting of Hitler, Mussolini, and Chamberlain to "two starving wolves [Hitler and Mussolini] sitting down to eat with an overstuffed Cornish hen [Chamberlain], only to discover there is no food on the table. Naturally, there is nothing left to do but to devour the English delicacy, which would certainly then call on Americans to join the festivities in the banquet hall." The long and the short of it was that there were hints of war in the air.

Not only was Europe cause for concern. Japanese and Chinese military forces were already trading shots in the air above and on the China Sea. "There is little doubt," noted one newspaper columnist, "that both of these powers [China and Japan] are putting together powerful military machinery, capable of waging battle upon each other or other nations."

Such was the news in Portland, Oregon, and the rest of the country on February 24, 1938, as Philip Knight made his appearance.

AMERICANS SEEK ENJOYMENT

Most Americans, however, were not greatly concerned with events that were happening thousands of miles from home. They were more concerned with pulling themselves out of the economic depression that gripped the country and were looking for happier times.

"What's playing at the Bijou Theatre? I hope it's 'Curlylocks'!"

That's a question that could easily have been asked in many a Portland home in February of 1938. "Curlylocks" was Shirley Temple, of course! With a smile and a pout that melted the hearts of everyone, the ten-year-old child movie star danced and sang her way to the bank each year with an unbelievable $300,000! In 1938, she ranked as the nation's favorite movie star, beating out leading man Clark Gable.

"Who's the 'Brown Bomber' scheduled to fight next?"

That's another question that could easily have been asked in Portland on February 24, 1938. As anyone who had any knowledge about sports knew, the "Brown Bomber" was heavyweight boxing champion Joe Louis. The night before, Louis had knocked out Nathan Mann in the third round. Who would be Louis' next opponent? A 15-round bout with Harry Thomas of Eagle Bend, Minnesota was already scheduled for April 1 in Chicago's Stadium.

Peace negotiations in London, skirmishes over the China Sea, Shirley Temple at the movies, Joe Louis in the boxing ring—these were the people and events capturing the news headlines on Thursday, February 24, 1938. But those events and newsmakers were far from the minds of William and Lota Hatfield Knight in Portland, Oregon. As far as they were concerned, there was only one newsmaker on that day, and he captured attention by displaying a healthy set of lungs in a Portland hospital.

His name was Philip Knight.

Chapter 3

Off to School

Like millions of other Americans, the family of William Knight was fast asleep during the early morning hours of Sunday, December 7, 1941. Three-year-old Philip had become caught up in the bright lights and fancy Christmas displays in the Portland department stores. Although too young to understand the forthcoming holidays, he nevertheless sensed that something special was on the way. But on this particular day, the boy slept peacefully, unaware of the stark drama unfolding faraway in the Pacific.

UNDER ATTACK

High above the Hawaiian island of Oahu, Japanese pilots studied their targets below. It was shortly before 7 A.M., and the American military personnel stationed at Pearl Harbor were just waking up.

Suddenly it happened. Bomb after bomb began emerging

from the Japanese planes, dropping through the air, and exploding on the American ships moored in the harbor below. Area military airports were attacked, too. Still dazed with sleep, soldiers and sailors hurried to man their positions.

Explosion after explosion ripped the Pearl Harbor naval base, sending waves of flame and smoke into the overhead sky. Again and again, the Japanese pilots dipped and glided their planes through the air, releasing their cargo of death and destruction.

As radio stations in the United States interrupted their regular Sunday morning programming to bring news of the bombing of Pearl Harbor, most Americans shook their heads in disbelief. It wasn't as if the news came as a complete shock in many households. In the past few years, the world had watched as Japan, Germany, and Italy had methodically built up arsenals of military might. Countries in Europe and Asia had been blatantly attacked, then swallowed up by these aggressors. But an open attack on the United States? It did not seem possible.

False Alarm

Years before, a man named Orson Welles had broadcast a special radio show on Halloween night. "The War of the Worlds" dealt with a supposed invasion of Earth by people from another planet. Despite frequent announcements that the program was totally fiction, a tale by H. G. Wells, countless listeners thought the country had really been attacked.

Because a hint of war was already in the air, it did not take much of this false alarm to trigger the imagination of many people. Some listeners packed their bags and left their homes to find safety. Others boarded themselves in so no aliens could get them.

A NATION AT WAR

But the events on December 7, 1941, were not fiction. The news announcements about Pearl Harbor were very real. The next day, President Roosevelt called Congress together and spelled out details of "the day that would live in infamy." With memories of World War I still lingering in the minds of William and Lota Knight and millions of other Americans, once again the United States was called into battle.

For young Philip Knight, however, America's entry into World War II had little impact. While American military forces waged battle in lands far from the United States, Philip enjoyed the safety and security of a loving home. His weapons were toys and blocks. And the only battles he knew about were those fought against the "bad guys" by cowboy heroes like Roy Rogers and Gene Autry on the nation's movie screens.

SCHOOL KIDS HELP OUT

But once in school, Philip was indeed touched by World War II. Across the country, school children proudly purchased defense stamps. There were red stamps that sold for ten cents and green stamps that cost twenty-five cents. Once purchased, the stamps were carefully pasted into booklets that were traded in for war bonds when completely filled. It was a good way of having children save money for the future while making them feel important helping out the war effort.

When Philip was seven and enjoying elementary school, the war ended. As the soldiers and sailors came home, the country returned to normal. School classrooms buzzed with news of dads, brothers, and sisters returning to their homes from faraway places.

APPRECIATING THE GREAT NORTHWEST

Like his classmates, Philip heard stories about the local Willamette River Valley, once inhabited only by Indians. These people lived quietly off the land, following the traditions of their ancestors. In time, trappers and settlers came to this region of the West for its rich bounty.

The Indian trails leading to the Willamette River were widened into roads so that settlers could reach Portland, the fastest-growing city in the Northwest. The dark, fertile soil in the valley attracted farmers, and soon orchards dotted the territory as well. Vineyards also flourished, their giant grape clusters producing the juice for fine wines.

As a boy growing up, Philip Knight learned to love the people and places where he lived. He vowed that it would always be his home, no matter what he did with his life in the years ahead.

SCHOOL DAYS

But for now, there were games and toys and fun and friends. There were new words to learn each day at school, as well as math and science, history and geography. Not that Philip completely immersed himself in his studies. Like the other boys, he also enjoyed his free time as well.

"What's your favorite time in school?"

"Recess!" was the most frequent answer.

"Don't you like anything else about school?"

"Hm-m-m . . ." A long pause. "I guess lunchtime is okay, too."

Such was the chatter between boys growing up in the 1940s and their elders. It is an exchange of words that has changed little over the generations.

CHANGES, CHANGES

How young Philip's eyes widened at the sight of the first television set brought into the Knight house. By 1949, Americans were buying 100,000 sets a week. The younger set was laughing at the antics of Howdy-Doody and Buffalo Bob, while also thrilling to the adventures of a cheerful cowboy on a white horse—Hopalong Cassidy. "Hoppy" clothing grossed $40 million in 1950!

Approaching his teens, Philip Knight entered junior high school with the beginning of a new decade. American soldiers again headed across the sea to fight in a place called Korea. Philip sat in classrooms learning about President Harry Truman, then President Dwight D. Eisenhower. The math courses became more advanced—algebra and geometry—and students were introduced to Charles Dickens and William Shakespeare.

Always, however, there was time to "mess around"—to go to football and basketball games, plays, and dances. And there was rock and roll, music that could never be turned up loud enough and that drove adults crazy. At the movies, John Wayne and Errol Flynn filled the screen with daring adventures, just as Philip and his pals longed to have their own lives filled with more excitement. Friends were vital, with some breaking off into couples, willing to suffer the fun and frustrations of teenage romances.

A LOVE OF RUNNING

By the time Philip reached high school, he had grown into a young man whose smile came quickly and who enjoyed running. But his thoughts about a future occupation or profession were still somewhat vague. Business seemed likely, in some form or another, but for now it was running that took up much of his interest and time.

However, there was a problem with running. Much as Philip loved the feel of stretching and testing his body—its speed, coordination, and endurance—the experience was painful. Often, when he returned after a long run and removed his shoes, he discovered that his sore and tired feet were actually bleeding. Philip wondered why. Was it really necessary to suffer like this?

But despite the hurt and physical suffering, Philip was not inclined to give up doing something that offered him so much challenge. However, he felt that surely there was something that could be done to lessen—or even remove—the pain that accompanied running. It was a thought that kept Philip Knight awake at night.

Chapter 4

A Fateful Meeting

His high school diploma tucked securely away, Philip Knight stood ready to enter the halls of higher education. In the fall of 1955, he enrolled at the University of Oregon, in Eugene. About a hundred miles from Portland, the distance offered Philip a chance to be on his own and still return home whenever he wanted. Anyway, he had little desire to leave the Northwest.

COLLEGE LIFE

Philip knew that college was a different way of life. At college, one assumed greater personal responsibility. There were no mothers and fathers looking over your shoulder to make you study. Studying was done independently. And as Philip sat in at a freshman meeting to learn about the university's rules and regulations, he heard words spoken that are the same at college campuses all across the country.

"Of you freshmen sitting in the audience today, only one out of three of you will complete your degree requirements." The speaker paused, effectively letting his jarring statement sink in. "That's the general percentage, the average. Are you going to be the one who makes it? That is basically up to you."

Philip Knight had not entered college to flunk out. He took his studies seriously. For some time he had been interested in business, so he took every business course he could get. And whether the course was Basic Business Principles or Advanced Accounting, Philip worked hard to keep his grades up.

But even though he studied hard, Philip was not about to give up running. It kept him in shape, cleared his mind from frustrations and stress, and gave him special goals to shoot for, such as improving his time and endurance. Still, this was one "Duck" (the nickname for a student at the University of Oregon) who sometimes wished he had webbed feet so he could run without suffering any pain.

ENTER BILL BOWERMAN

Philip Knight wasn't the only individual at the University of Oregon who was unhappy about running shoes. Bill Bowerman was, too. As head track coach at the school, Bowerman knew that the shoes worn by athletes were simply not all that good. They lacked cushioning and were too heavy.

Unlike others who felt the same way, Bowerman decided to do something about the situation instead of just complain about it. He carefully designed a shoe with better traction and support. Then he sent his ideas off to every sporting-goods company in the country.

Some of the replies were longer than others, and some were more courteous. But in every case the final answer was a resounding "No thanks!"

Putting "Competitive Response" into Action

However, Bill Bowerman would not give up. As a coach, he preached a philosophy of "competitive response" to his athletes. He did not want his runners to seek only tangible rewards—ribbons or medals—but rather, he also wanted them to attain personal victories, mentally and spiritually. "A hard-fought loss can be more beneficial than a no-effort victory," he would tell his trackmen. Both winning and losing could prove useful. In losing, it was essential to understand why it happened so that it wouldn't happen again.

Applying "competitive response" to his own situation, Bowerman decided that if the sporting-goods companies would not make his shoes, he'd make them himself. And he did just that. With a bunch of old grocery bags, Bowerman sketched and cut out different patterns, constantly shaping them into streamlined designs. Then he put together his first pairs of actual shoes. Lightweight and sleek, they were eagerly accepted by members of his track team.

Compared to other brands, Bowerman's shoes may have looked a bit less stylish. But the running Ducks of Oregon did not care what the shoes looked like. They offered more support and the runners clocked better times. Philip Knight improved his own running times, reducing his mile to four minutes and thirteen seconds (4:13). Not bad for a middle distance man!

A STINT IN THE ARMY

In 1959, Philip Knight graduated from the University of Oregon with a bachelor's degree in business administration. He then went into the United States Army, where he served on active duty with the Transportation Corps and worked himself up to first lieutenant.

After leaving the Army in 1960, Knight headed for Stanford University, a school in California well known for its business programs. In one class, Knight was asked to set up plans for a small business. On paper, he laid out an imaginary shoe company and the framework for setting it up.

The young graduate student's research was clear and concise. At the time, Japanese manufacturers were taking over the camera business, slipping by other foreign competitors and American manufacturers. Why couldn't the Japanese do the same thing with athletic shoes? In Knight's opinion, they could.

A TRIP ABROAD

As soon as he graduated from Stanford in 1962 with a master's degree, Knight went on a world tour. While in Tokyo, he called on the executives of the Onitsuka Company, which manufactured the popular Tiger running shoes. Under pressure to appear as an experienced businessman, Knight labeled himself the owner of "Blue Ribbon Sports" back home.

The Japanese officials were impressed by Knight and his ideas. By the time he returned home, Philip had been authorized by Onitsuka to be the sole distributor of its Tiger running shoes in

America. Now, all he needed was $1,000 to cover the first order. If only he could find a partner to share expenses.

The Return of Bill Bowerman

Philip Knight did not have to think long. How well he remembered his former track coach at the University of Oregon. No one else had greater recognition of the need for better running shoes in America than Bill Bowerman.

Meeting in Bowerman's kitchen, the two men hammered out the details of their business arrangement. Each would put up $500 to cover initial expenses. The Onitsuka Company was also eager to hear about Bowerman's ideas for improving running shoes.

A STORE IN A CAR TRUNK

In December of 1963, the first shipment of Tiger running shoes arrived in Oregon. Thankfully, William Knight's basement had enough room to store the 200 pairs of shoes.

Since Philip was now working for a local accounting firm, he could only sell the shoes during his spare time. At every opportunity, he loaded the shoes into his car trunk and headed for local and regional track meets. There he stood, eager and willing to accommodate coaches and runners as they came to his car. In 1964, Blue Ribbon Sports (actually, Philip Knight and Bill Bowerman) sold 1,300 pairs of Tiger running shoes, taking in $8,000 in **revenues.**

During the following year, Blue Ribbon Sports added an employee. Jeff Johnson, a former track competitor of Philip's, was impressed with what Knight and Bowerman had accomplished. He decided to give up his job selling Adidas football shoes and climb aboard the Blue Ribbon Sports wagon. In doing so, Johnson became

runners coming in fourth, fifth, sixth, and seventh wore Nikes. A shrewd Philip Knight developed an advertising campaign boasting that four out of the top seven marathoners at the Olympic trials wore Nike running shoes. Across the country, professional and amateur runners took notice.

TROUBLES OVERSEAS

But as Nike captured the attention of athletes in America, Philip Knight's business colleagues at Onitsuka began causing problems. A court case confirmed that the Japanese company had established a separate distribution network in America for its Tiger-brand shoes. Attempts to resolve the problems in court failed. Quickly, Philip Knight boarded a plane and flew to Japan. But the troubles could not be ironed out and Onitsuka cut off all shipments to Knight's company.

There was not a moment to waste. Orders for Nike products were coming in rapidly. Delays meant unhappy customers and cancelled orders. But Philip Knight had done his research and already knew of other possible manufacturers for his goods. Within thirty days, he had lined up a new manufacturer. The world of Nike was again secure.

"RUBBER WAFFLES"

In the meantime, Bill Bowerman continued to search for new ways to improve Nike shoes. "I was pleased with what we'd done," explained Bowerman, "but never convinced that we couldn't do better." The veteran track coach felt that a runner who carried one extra ounce of weight for a mile was like carrying an extra thousand pounds in the last fifty yards of a distance race. Determined to design the lightest shoe possible, Bowerman continued experimenting.

Suddenly, Bill Bowerman got the idea of a waffle-patterned sole. To test his thinking, he poured some urethane rubber into the family waffle iron one Sunday morning. When he finished, it was clear that the waffle iron had heated its last waffle.

But the exciting result of Bowerman's experimenting was Nike's first revolutionary discovery. The tiny rubber studs of the waffle iron provided a newfound springiness to Nike shoes. Soon, the Moon Shoe with its waffle soles was delighting customers, especially the occasional runners so often pained by bruising.

From Frowns to Smiles

Philip Knight had worn few smiles at the beginning of 1972 because of the problems with Onitsuka. But by the end of that same year, he was smiling broadly. The company's revenues approached $2,000,000, forty-five people were working full time for Blue Ribbon Sports, and Canada became the first foreign market to handle company products. Not bad, thought thirty-four-year-old Philip Knight. Not bad at all.

Nike was now a familiar name among professional athletes. Steve Prefontaine, an American record holder in track, not only wore Nike shoes himself but encouraged fellow competitors to do the same. Jon Anderson won the rigorous Boston Marathon in a pair of Nike running shoes. Top-ranked tennis star Ilie Nastase dashed across the courts in a pair of Nikes.

The company's business department streamlined its ordering operation, enabling the company to "make to order" for its customers. Not only did this help the customers, it prevented the company from carrying too much **inventory.** To top things off, Philip and Penelope Knight welcomed their second son, Travis, in 1973.

As the country tried to recover from the resignation of President Richard Nixon, Nike continued its growth pattern in 1974. Exeter, New Hampshire, became the site for the first Blue Ribbon Sports manufacturing plant in the United States. Jimmy Connors scored tennis wins at both Wimbledon and the U.S. Open, wearing—of course!—Nike shoes. And he wasn't even under company contract! Australia joined the Blue Ribbon Sports retailing network, while the company's annual revenues climbed toward $5,000,000.

THE JOGGING CRAZE

There is little doubt that Nike fortunes were greatly enhanced by the jogging craze that swept America during the mid-1970s. Health- and exercise-conscious people of every shape and size took up running. People who were not athletes and cared little about their times and endurance enjoyed jogging, and they wanted to look good while doing it.

Despite the demands of operating a company, Philip Knight maintained his own daily schedule for running, often jogging to and from work each day. It was a definite part of his own longtime health and exercise program, but it also gave him a chance to notice what shoes other joggers were wearing.

Nike continued to rack up historic milestones in the 1970s. Manufacturing operations were opened in Taiwan, Korea, and

In 1974, Philip Knight expanded the operations of Blue Ribbon Sports by opening the company's first manufacturing plant in Exeter, New Hampshire. (Richard Howard.)

another one in the United States. A children's line was introduced. It included Wally Waffle, Robbie Road Racer, and Burt Bruin shoes. Tennis star John McEnroe signed a contract to **endorse** Nike. And European distributors were lined up, helping to push revenues over the $100 million figure worldwide by the late 1970s.

NAME CHANGE

In 1978, Blue Ribbon Sports officially adopted Nike, Inc., as a corporate name. Too many people thought Blue Ribbon Sports and Nike were two separate companies. Philip Knight certainly wanted no confusion about that matter. In business, he knew the importance of quick and distinct name recognition. The following year, he took personal pride in opening the company's world headquarters in Beaverton, Oregon, a stone's throw from Portland. Truly, the hometown boy had made good.

The Country's Most Popular Running Shoes

At the beginning of the 1980s, Nike claimed the title as the most popular athletic shoe in America, with nearly half of all running shoe revenues. Not that *everyone* accepted the idea that Nike offered the best quality in shoes. *Runner's World* magazine gave Brooks Shoe Manufacturing Company higher rankings in its evaluations of running shoes, but Nike protested. Nike people charged that Brooks enjoyed close business links with *Runner's World,* which resulted in the favored rankings.

Could Nike continue its rapid climb into the 1980s? The jogging craze had already begun to show signs of dying out. Would that waning interest hurt Nike? There were people who complained that Nike prices were too high. Also, what about Adidas? And then there was a company named Reebok.

Now in his early forties, Philip Knight huffed and puffed a bit louder and longer after a long run. But he showed few signs of wearing out. Hardly. Often, he appeared to just be catching his second wind.

Then, watch out!

Chapter 6

"Just Do It!"

From the very beginning of his business life, Philip Knight knew it was important to show the public that he was concerned about their comfort and safety. "Anyone offering a product or service must keep the customer in mind," he noted at one business gathering. "That sounds so obvious, and yet it's easy to get caught up in the complexities of big business and forget the most important cog [the customer] in the wheel."

To kick off the 1980s, Knight announced that two million shares of Nike stock would be sold to the public. Soon, another announcement followed. A Nike Sports Research and Development Laboratory was to be opened at the manufacturing plant in Exeter. "We are committed to provide the best for professional athletes and those who simply enjoy sports as personal recreation," offered a company spokesperson.

The Importance of Quality

To be successful, any entrepreneur knows that he or she has to provide potential customers with a needed product or service. Philip Knight spotted a need for quality running shoes, for both the professional and the amateur runner.

Recognizing the immense popularity of jogging as a recreational pastime, Knight focused his main attention on developing better running shoes. But he was never one to put all of his eggs in one basket. "Don't be shy—diversify!" is the Nike philosophy, and that philosophy has paid off in rich dividends.

What began as a singular product line of running shoes has mushroomed into hundreds of offerings. In addition to many different types of shoes, Nike now sells a wide range of athletic equipment as well as stylish outfits for leisure activities.

"But no matter how many items you offer," observes Knight, "you have to give people quality. If a customer likes your brand of shoes, he's likely to give your brand of sweatshirt a look. The secret of success in winning customers is to offer them quality products."

GETTING BIGGER AND BIGGER

There was no doubt that Nike anticipated big business ahead. Negotiations were opened with the People's Republic of China to manufacture Nike shoes there. The shoes had already reached top-seller status in Canada. By the end of 1980, there were 2,700 Nike employees and revenues totaled $269 million.

By the following year, Nike goods were available in more than forty countries, and eleven of those nations had manufacturing facilities of their own. Nike International, Ltd., was formed to oversee foreign operations, while Nike-England became the company's first wholly-owned foreign distributorship. To provide retailers in the United States with quick personal and technical assistance, the company created Ekin (Nike spelled backwards), with representatives available across the country.

New products continued to appear—a basketball shoe labeled Air Force 1 and a tennis shoe called the Air Ace. Over 200 models were included in the Nike shoe line, while the Nike apparel line also approached 200 different offerings.

In recognition of his efforts and achievements, Philip Knight was named Oregon Businessman of the Year in 1982.

SUPPORTING THE OLYMPICS

Constantly growing, Nike was enjoying widespread popularity by 1984, when it helped promote the summer Olympics being held in the United States. Product, advertising, and marketing departments pooled their talents to produce eye-catching billboards in nine major

Despite hundreds of clothing items, the more than 200 models of Nike shoes are still the core of the company's multi-billion-dollar business. (Richard Howard.)

American cities. Fifty-eight Nike-supported athletes competed at the games, which were held in Los Angeles. The handsome lightning bolt insignia was seen everywhere.

The Nike-supported athletes carted home a total of 65 medals. Joan Benoit triumphed in the first women's Olympic marathon, while runner Carl Lewis captured four gold medals. On the surface, all seemed to be going well for Nike. Yet, by the end of the year, its stock had fallen some sixty percent in value. Clearly, something was wrong. As business people say, when corporations battle hard times, Nike had "hit the wall."

Watch Out for Reebok

One difficulty was largely beyond Nike's control. Jogging as a health and recreational activity had given way to aerobics. There was no controlling the exercising interests of the American public. Fashionable soft leather athletic shoes replaced the clunkier running shoes, especially for women who were caught up in "aerobicking." Reebok had always paid more attention to shoe style, while Nike had always emphasized shoe performance. Reebok had done a super job anticipating the demand for aerobic shoes, which Nike had not done.

MUSICAL CHAIRS

But there were some problems that Nike seemed to have brought on itself. Inside the company's executive offices, **management** seemed to be playing musical chairs. Philip Knight himself was one of the players.

For a while, Knight thrived on supervising the daily operations of the company. Then he chose to focus his attention on international operations. Others in the organization did the same, moving from spot to spot, from major interest to major interest. Jokes about the many changes circulated among employees around the company.

"Who's in charge of Nike marketing?" someone might ask.

"This month or next month?" would come the answer.

Rumors also began circulating that Philip Knight was not keeping tight enough rein on many of his top executives. Some were personal friends, former "jocks" who enjoyed a close friendship with Nike's chief yet lacked the managerial skills demanded of an international corporation.

Arrogance at the Top

Employees breathed a bit easier in 1985 when basketball's power and glory, the Chicago Bulls' superstar Michael Jordan, endorsed a Nike line of Air Jordan sportswear. Sales of the clothing skyrocketed. Millions of young Jordan fans wanted only what Michael put his name to.

Promoting a Product

"The best product, no matter how perfectly crafted and styled, is doomed to failure unless it is properly promoted." Philip Knight's words are put into action in the form of aggressive marketing campaigns, sparked largely by the Portland advertising agency of Wieden & Kennedy.

About three percent of Nike's annual sales revenue automatically goes for product promotion. That amounts to more than $70 million a year. Knight is convinced that professional athletes like Michael Jordan and Bo Jackson, or perhaps the whole defensive line of the Dallas Cowboys, are Nike's best advertisements.

Unlike glamorous still-life models, the use of active competitors in the daily sports spotlight suggests that they would not have attained their success without the help of top-flight Nike equipment. They appear in regular Nike ads, and when pictures of Jordan or Jackson also appear on the sports pages of newspapers and magazines, they capture a media spotlight that cannot be bought.

Knight is fully aware that amateur athletes notice what their idols are wearing. "If Michael Jordan can win with those shoes," thinks John Q. Public, "maybe I can, too." It's exactly that kind of thinking that fills the Nike cash registers.

"You put a pair of Nike shoes on the right pair of feet and they get noticed," Knight affirms. Sales figures back up his claim. Clearly, "action advertising" sells Nike.

But the sales flurry was short-lived. Soon the rumors began circulating again. There was talk that Nike's chief competitor, Reebok International, had taken over the lead in 1986. Then, when actual sales figures became known, talk became fact. Although

Nike's revenues were over a billion dollars for 1986, Reebok had passed Nike, capturing thirty percent of the market to NIKE's twenty-one percent.

But how?

"Arrogance" was the term Philip Knight used. "We went through a number of years where we predicted the market with astonishing accuracy. We got a little arrogant. Then everything changed."

MAKING A COMEBACK

Eager to make a comeback, Knight carefully analyzed the situation. Reebok had made the most of customer interest in styles and fashions. So be it. The Nike chieftain had no intention of trying to anticipate the fashion business from year to year. "We have to concentrate on making the best-quality, best-performing shoes we can," he insisted.

But there were definite steps that Philip Knight could take, and like it or not, he took them. He slashed **overhead** costs, closing factories in the United States and elsewhere that were no longer needed. Nearly all production orders were sent to contractors in South Korea, Taiwan, and Thailand, where labor and materials were cheaper. Over 1,000 employees were dropped, including some top executives. Stronger lines of communication between design, marketing, and production were established. Advertising and **promotional** costs were cut twenty percent. And although Knight wasn't interested in fashion trend-setting, he made it clear that bright colors and fashion touches would be woven into existing and future Nike products. To broaden its offerings, Nike acquired Cole-Haan, a manufacturer of men's and women's dress and casual footwear.

In the Lead Again

By 1988, thanks largely to Knight's changes, the spotlight was again on Nike as the technological and financial leader of the sports-shoe industry. Nike-Air had become more than a brand name—it was now a household word. With each addition to the Michael Jordan line of shoes and apparel, sales figures climbed. It was clear that one of Philip Knight's wisest moves was to secure the services of basketball's "king of the court."

Simplicity is always a key ingredient of content and style. Philip Knight explored its use further with marketing. Utilizing the services of Los Angeles Raider and Kansas City Royal standout Bo Jackson, the advertising whizzes at Nike successfully put the super athlete's talents to work. The simple phrase, "Bo Knows," became one of the most popular—and easily recognizable— commercials of the late 1980s. Standing by its side was the "Just Do It" theme, emphasizing to anyone that anything is possible if you "just do it." (That is, if you're using Nike products!)

"Quality products, classy marketing and advertising—Nike has it all," observed a rival in the industry. "You have to run pretty fast to keep up with them, and if you can, you'd probably be running in Nike shoes."

BUILDING FOR THE FUTURE

Needless to say, Philip Knight was happy to see Nike on top of the sales charts by the end of the 1980s. How long and far he had traveled since those early days of Blue Ribbon Sports, when he drove around to track meets selling shoes out of the trunk of his car.

In 1989, he was named Man of the Year by *Footwear News,* the shoe industry's leading publication.

Now, at his desk, the head of Nike admired the plans for the company's new international headquarters that would soon sprawl gracefully over 74 acres in Beaverton. It seemed only right that the complex would be located at One Bowerman Drive.

As he looked at the plans, Philip Knight reflected proudly on the growth of his company over the past twenty-six years. He had met and overcome problems while leading the company to a position of prominence in the business world. Unfortunately, he had no knowledge of events taking place elsewhere that would soon embroil Nike in great controversy.

Chapter 7

When PUSH Comes to Shove

Summers are hot in Chicago. And during the summer of 1990, temperatures soared even hotter—especially inside the walls of PUSH headquarters at 930 E. 50th Street. It was not the air temperature that bothered the civil rights workers inside the building; air conditioners provided relief against that heat.

No, the PUSH people were putting their own heat on Nike in the form of an all-out **boycott** campaign of the company's products. "Our organization attempts to avoid direct action of this nature," offered Reverend Tyrone Crider, National Executive Director of Operation PUSH. "But the actions of Nike officials offer us no other choice in this matter. If we cannot **negotiate** peacefully at the **bargaining table,** we will wage an attack at the cash register."

This declaration of a **consumer** war captured headlines

across the country. Both PUSH and Nike were familiar names in the nation's households. "What's all the fuss about?" people wondered.

THE PUSH ORGANIZATION

Founded on Christmas Day in 1971, Operation PUSH (People United to Serve Humanity) was captained by the Reverend Jesse Jackson and seventy other diverse leaders. The main goal of the organization centered around economic cooperation between the American business community and African-Americans. It also sought to add political power for blacks through increased voter registration and education. PUSH even hoped it could help de-escalate the nuclear arms race.

Under Jackson's leadership, PUSH claimed success in a variety of areas. Jobs for minorities were increased by integrating **trade unions,** minorities became more visible in the broadcast media, and general fairness between minorities and whites in sports competition was advanced.

When Jesse Jackson launched a bid for the American presidency in 1984, the first black man to do so as a major political party candidate, PUSH shared some of the spotlight with its founder. Jackson garnered over 3,000,000 votes in various state primaries. Four years later, he ran again, winning over 6,000,000 votes in state primaries. Again, PUSH won wide public attention.

But it was in the realm of business negotiations that PUSH claimed its greatest successes as a civil rights organization. Through the PUSH International Trade Bureau (PITB), improved employment opportunities for blacks and other minorities were achieved with such major companies as Burger King, Seven-Up, Kentucky-Fried Chicken, Coca-Cola, and Ford Motor Company.

NIKE'S TURN

Now it was Nike's turn. As the leader in the production of athletic shoes, Nike attracted a large number of African-American customers. According to PUSH figures, Nike sold $200 million worth of footwear to blacks each year. This represented thirty percent of the company's total sales. PUSH hoped to develop a stronger **reciprocal** economic relationship between blacks and Nike.

A Meeting with PUSH

At its 19th Annual National Convention in Chicago on July 22–25, 1990, PUSH Director Crider announced plans to target Nike for its failure to help African-Americans achieve economic **parity** within the company. Richard Donahue, Nike's **chief executive officer (CEO),** agreed to cooperate, and representatives of the two organizations met in Chicago on July 31, during the National Sporting Goods Exposition.

All seemed to go well. As Donahue noted, "This was not an adversarial proceeding [a meeting between enemies]. PUSH has made a point and we intend to respond to it." In his briefcase, Donahue carried a questionnaire from the PUSH organization requesting data about African-American and other minority representation in various capacities within Nike. After his return to Beaverton, Donahue immediately went into conference with Philip Knight.

A Defiant Knight

Knight little appreciated the PUSH tactics. Coca-Cola, Kentucky-Fried Chicken, and the other companies might feel intimidated by the People United to Serve Humanity, but Philip Knight was proud of Nike, its people, and its products. He did not like pressure tactics. With defiance, he challenged the PUSH figures regarding the percentage of sales to African-Americans and the money they spent on Nike products. "Grossly inflated!" observed Philip Knight.

A deadline of August 10 had been set for Nike to complete and return the PUSH questionnaire. The date came and went. Still no word came from Nike headquarters. By the middle of August, PUSH issued a list of demands to Nike—employ more blacks, reserve at least one seat on the Nike **board of directors** for a black, use black advertising agencies, and hire black lawyers.

Shoving Back

With PUSH pushing, Nike shoved right back. Philip Knight fired off a twenty-one-page letter demanding an accounting of PUSH finances. In 1988, after three years of having his organization's financial records checked by the United States government, PUSH leader Jesse Jackson agreed to pay $550,000 to settle a federal claim. Federal **auditors** said they had evidence of undocumented expenditures of over $6,000,000 from government grants and contracts that had been awarded to PUSH.

A question was also raised about Reebok's purchase of advertising in a PUSH magazine. Could that have influenced PUSH's decision to publicly attack Nike?

Temperatures Rise

Ordinarily, summer is a relatively peaceful season in the business world. But as accusations, insinuations, and questions heated the air, consumer spectators viewed a unique squabble. Philip Knight was never known to pick a fight, but neither was he a person to back away from one. He was proud of his company, and he was not about to let anyone attack it, especially with incorrect facts and figures. But he wanted no confusion about whom the battle was between.

"Let's make sure one point is clearly understood," Knight asserted. "This is not a fight between Nike and blacks. This is a disagreement between Nike and PUSH."

The PUSH organization also wanted to make sure the public knew that black spokespersons who endorsed Nike products were free from blame. Basketball star Michael Jordan, football great Bo Jackson, coach John Thompson, actor/director Spike Lee, and other blacks who were associated with Nike enjoyed wide popularity across the nation.

"We have no complaint with any of these individuals," stated PUSH officials. "They are positive role models from our community who promote Nike products. They have nothing to do with setting Nike corporate policy, which is what is at issue here."

Saying No to Nike

Carefully, PUSH leaders mounted a boycott campaign. Potential customers were asked to refrain from buying Nike products. Those who already owned Nike products were asked to put black tape over the name and the lightning bolt emblem. Leaflets and petitions supporting the boycott were printed and circulated. Speakers were encouraged to visit television talk shows and discuss the situation, while others were encouraged to send letters to the editors of their local newspapers and magazines.

"It's vital that the public know what's going on," declared planners of the boycott. "People must be educated or our mission is wasted."

A program was set up to visit retail store owners with a request that Nike products be withdrawn. Finally, supporters of the boycott were asked to write personally to Knight, stating their objections to his corporate policies.

CHOOSING SIDES

There were many who felt PUSH was overreacting or perhaps taking a negative low road. On the weekly television show "The McLaughlin Group," journalist Morton Kondrake suggested that if Jesse Jackson had really wanted to get something done for blacks through Nike, he might simply have called Philip Knight and proposed John Thompson as a member of the company's board of directors. Instead, it had to become "a big publicity gimmick."

Over breakfast and lunch, businessmen across the nation buzzed about the boycott. Some supported the PUSH campaign, while others stood firmly in the Nike camp.

Among the boycott supporters were black leaders Dr. Benjamin Hooks, Martin Luther King III, and even boxing promoter Don King. The United Mine Workers of America, the National Urban Coalition, and the Hispanic Association for Corporate Responsibility were organizations that signed up against Nike policies.

Many newspapers deplored the PUSH tactics. "Philip Knight just happens to be a creative and shrewd entrepreneur, an individual who built a blockbuster of a business virtually from scratch," one editorial declared. "To smear him and his corporation for not playing fair with blacks is ridiculous! It is well known that Nike has supported many worthwhile African-American causes."

PUSH admitted that Nike had given money to African-American causes. "But that was in line with their desire to present a good corporate image," insisted PUSH leaders. "What we are concerned with is not charity but rather economic parity."

A BIG ZERO

"But why a boycott?" critics of the PUSH campaign asked.

"We are using our legitimate consumer rights to combat the 'zero' factor policies in place at Nike," PUSH officials answered. "At Nike, ZERO African-Americans hold key executive positions; ZERO African-American-owned television stations, radio stations, newspapers, and magazines carry Nike advertisements; and where the services of ZERO African-American-owned law firms, insurance agencies, advertising agencies, financial service firms, banks, and other professional service providers are being utilized. It is these apartheid corporate policies that we object to and are working to dismantle."

"Apartheid." Now there was a term sure to fan the flames of the ever-growing fire, as if the summer was not already hot enough. Most Americans associated the term with the brutal, white-supremist business and political structure of South Africa. Surely such a practice did not operate within the free enterprise system of the United States! Or did it?

AN ATTEMPT AT
AFFIRMATIVE ACTION

There were certainly no apartheid policies at Nike in the thinking of Philip Knight and the company's collective leadership. The charge was outrageous! But as a show of concern and goodwill, an **affir-**

mative action announcement was released by the Nike people. The company agreed to add a "minority" to their board of directors and a "minority" vice-president within the next twenty-four months.

The PUSH reply was swift. "Such affirmative action is inadequate and does not fall within an acceptable time frame. It did not take Nike twenty-four months to find Michael Jordan. It should not take them twenty-four months to find qualified executives. The announcement also left open Nike's definition of the term 'minority.' Furthermore, their announcement did not address **procurement** opportunities for African-American-owned businesses and professional service firms."

NO COMPROMISES

Philip Knight sat in his office in Beaverton shaking his head. There seemed to be no way of satisfying PUSH. The organization did not make requests; it made demands. There would be no compromising. Everything Knight had accomplished in his life he had achieved with honesty and purpose, an ability to recognize a need and fill it, a desire to set goals and reach for them.

Yet sometimes there was a need to make compromises in business. This did not mean the sacrificing of principles, however. As a businessman, more importantly as a person, Philip Knight stood for something. Integrity was not just a remote thought or idea. It was a code that he tried to live by.

In the end, the problems with PUSH simply just disappeared. For some reason, the organization quietly ended its boycott efforts and ceased making further demands of Nike. In his battle with PUSH, Philip Knight refused to be cowed. He stuck by everything he believed in—and won!

Chapter 8

Into the Future

The summer of 1990 was certainly not one that Philip Knight would remember with great pleasure. "Philip is not a man who appreciates being attacked unfairly," noted one business associate. "He is proud of Nike, and the thought that he has ever mistreated or is improperly using any people in any way hurts him."

THE COLLEGE THAT NIKE BUILT

But it was a smiling Philip Knight who witnessed the official opening of the new 74-acre Nike, Inc., World Campus in Beaverton. The complex is somewhat like a small college. Handsome, reflective glass buildings stand guard around a man-made lake, surrounded by woods and encircled by (what else?) a 1½-mile jogging trail.

Within the confines of this corporate complex, some 2,700

No wonder Philip Knight is smiling, with Nike, Inc., reaching toward three billion dollars in annual revenues. (Chester Higgins/NYT Pictures.)

people work to keep Nike the "largest sneaker maker" in the world, among the company's other achievements. Annual revenues in 1980 topped $269 million. A decade later, in 1990, the figure stood at $2.2 billion. And by the year 2000—who knows?

But Philip Knight seems little driven by a desire to make more money. Not that he does not appreciate the financial success of Nike. Instead, he constantly seeks ways of improving Nike products through study and research.

THE DREAMER—AND DOER

As Philip Knight approaches a new century, it is with a sense of satisfaction and fulfilled purpose. More than a dreamer, he is a doer—one who recognized a special need and filled it. Nike stands as a living monument for what man can achieve through creative thinking, sound business practices, and a willingness to reach for the best.

And with the pride in his company and its family, Philip Knight considers himself fortunate in having married Penelope Parks and being blessed with two sons, Matthew and Travis. His parents, other family members, and friends also share treasured positions among those to whom he is greatly indebted.

As for advice to young business entrepreneurs, Philip Knight condenses his thoughts into a brief but wise statement: "Set goals for yourself, then work for them. Just do it!"

Glossary

affirmative action   Positive efforts made by an organization to hire and treat all of its employees equally, regardless of sex, race, religion, or nationality.

auditor   A person who examines financial records in order to determine their accuracy.

bargaining table   A place where differences are discussed in order to reach an agreement.

board of directors   A group of individuals, elected by shareholders, who set the policies and goals for a company.

boycott   A refusal to deal with or purchase goods from a company.

brokers   People who buy and sell stock, real estate, etc., for other people.

chief executive officer (CEO)   The executive in an organization who is responsible for carrying out the policies of the organization's board of directors.

competitor   In business, a company that sells the same product or services as other companies.

consumer   One who purchases goods or utilizes services.

contract   A legal agreement between two or more parties for doing something.

credit   A promise to pay for goods or services or to repay money borrowed at some specified future time.

depression   A long period of low economic activity, with much unemployment.

endorse   To approve of or support something, sometimes for a fee.

entrepreneur   A person who organizes, controls, and takes all the risk of running a business.

inventory   Merchandise or stock on hand.

investors   People who put money into something in the hopes of making more money (a profit) in the future.

management   The people who direct, control, or regulate the various operations of a business.

market   A specific group of consumers, such as teenagers or athletes, who will buy certain products or services.

marketing The various methods used by a company to sell its products or services.

merchandise Items that are sold to the general public.

negotiate To discuss a problem or an issue in order to reach an agreement.

overhead Such costs of running a business as rent, heat, electricity, taxes, and insurance; does not include the costs of making and selling the company's products.

parity Equality in value, status, or price.

policy A general plan or course of action.

procurement Getting or acquiring something, such as a contract to do work or provide services for a company.

promotion An activity a company uses to gain public awareness of its products or services.

reciprocal A fair exchange; an equal relationship of give and take.

retail The selling of goods to the general public.

revenue The money that a business takes in from the sale of its products or services.

spokesperson One who speaks for company management or endorses a company's products.

stock A certificate (share) of ownership in a company.

trade union An organization of workers in a business or industry.

trademark A distinguishing symbol or feature associated with a particular product.

Index